Unpacking Your Life's Purpose

Peter Wescombe

My mind is a centre of Divine operation. The Divine operation is always for expansion and fuller expression, and this means the production of something beyond what has gone before, something entirely new, not included in past experience, though proceeding out of it by an orderly sequence of growth. Therefore, since the Divine cannot change its inherent nature, it must operate in the same manner within me; consequently, in my own special world, of which I am the centre, it will move forward to produce new conditions, always in advance of any that have gone before.

Thomas Troward

Unpacking Your Life's Purpose

Living Authentically by Aligning How You Live with Who You Are.

Peter Wescombe

Wescombe Publishing

All rights reserved; no part of this book may be reproduced, stored in a retrieval system or transmitted in any form, or by any means, electronic, mechanical, photocopying, recording, or otherwise for public of private use – other than for "fair use" as brief quotations embodied in articles and reviews, without prior written permission of the publisher

The author does not dispense medical advice or prescribe the use of any technique as a form of treatment for physical or medical problems without the advice of a physician, either directly or indirectly. The intent of the author is only to offer information of a general nature to help you in your quest for emotional and spiritual well-being. In the event that you use any of the information in this book for yourself, which is your constitutional right, the author and publisher assume no responsibility for your actions.

For information, or to reach out to us in person, please contact us via email or visit our website

info@mountrolandretreat.com.au

https://mountrolandretreat.com.au

Copyright © 2024 Wescombe Publishing

All rights reserved.

ISBN: 978-1-7635693-0-0

Contents

Introduction	9
What Does "Life's Purpose" Mean?	15
Why Does it Matter?	19
Trusting in Your Life's Purpose	23
Clues to Discovering Your Life's Purpose	27
Core Values and Beliefs	28
Passions, Desires, and Ambitions	35
Interests and Curiosity	37
Listening to Your Heart and Connecting to Source Energy	38
Living in the Moment	39
Moments of Flow and Fulfillment.	41
What Energizes You, and What Drains You?	41
Milestones, Patterns and Pivotal Moments	43
Hobbies, Free-time Activities, and Volunteer Projects	44
What do Your Friends and Family Say About You?	45
Natural Gifts, Talents, and Abilities	46
Allow Yourself to Dream and Imagine	47
Experimenting with Different Paths and Activities	48
Hindrances and Blocks to Discovering Your Life's Purpose	51
Negative Religious Connotations with Life's Purpose	52
Mindsets and Limiting Beliefs	53
Arguing for Your Limitations	54
Fear of the Unknown, and Autonomic Nervous System Responses.	55
Fear of Rejection or Failure	56
External Pressures	57

Lack of Self-confidence and Self-worth	57
Opting Out of the Hamster Wheel Lifestyle	58
Procrastination vs Making a Decision to Do it Now	59
Lack of Clarity and Direction	60
Current Occupation and/or Skills	61
Victim Mentality	62
Lack of Self-love and Self-care	63
It's too Risky, and I'll Never Make Money Living My Life's Purpose.	64

Living Your Life's Purpose — 67

Power of Intention	68
Magic of Synchro-destiny and the Law of Attraction	71
Connecting with Source Energy	72
Your Mind is a Good Servant but a Bad Master	73
Overcoming Limiting Mindsets and Changing the Concept You Have of Yourself	76
Transitioning from Where you Are to Where you Want to Be	79
Take a Chance on Me – How Risky Is It Really?	85
Making Decisions and 7 Ways to Test Your Decision	87
Be You - Be Unstoppable - Be Obsessed!	92
Listening to Your Body and Its Feelings	95
Purpose, Visions, Goals, and Plans – How Does it All Fit Together?	96
Assessing Your Progress	99

Conclusion — 101

Introduction

This purpose of this book is to provide you with some clarity and simplicity in discovering and living your life on purpose. It sheds light on this hazy, and often neglected area of our lives, offering practical tips and strategies to guide you towards your north star and living your life authentically. This book is not meant to be an in-depth study or a comprehensive instructional study course. It is not the next "shiny new object" in the spiritual and personal development space. It's simply a guide to help you in discovering and exploring more about your wonderful life and your purpose on this planet.

It's also about building harmony and unity with all humanity rather than a divisive polarized energy where everyone is striving to show that their belief is right – whether it's religion, politics, personal development gurus, tools, techniques, modalities, or whatever. As the wise Native American proverb states, *"No tree has branches so foolish as to fight among themselves."* We all came from the same life source, we're all still connected to the same life source, and yet, here we are, after all this time, still not getting it, and still living as though we are strangers and in competition with each other.

Having said that, if there's one thing I've learned in life, it's the fact that no two people are the same. In the words of Carl Jung, *"The shoe that fits one person pinches another; there is no recipe for living that suits all cases."* Whether it's our physicality, our emotional makeup, our points of view, our concept of ourselves, our beliefs, gifts, talents, wants, dreams, and the many other aspects of our DNA and environmental evolvement, it's all about variety and uniqueness. We are each born as an authentically unique human being with a desire for full expression and expansion of that uniqueness. Like in nature; every plant, bush, and tree grows, expands, and expresses itself as fully and uniquely as it possibly can. Unfortunately, unlike the plant kingdom, once we humans "grow up" and "get control" of our lives, we tend to put limitations on ourselves, carefully constructing ceilings, safety zones, and parameters for our lives. We turn down the dials on our mind-set thermostat, settling for "moderate," "mediocre," "normal" and "average." These "sensible" adjustments we make to our lives act like dams, restricting the free flow of the life's powerful energy that yearns to course through us. Consequently, most people live way below their full potential, missing out on the rich, rewarding and fulfilling lives that are well within their grasp.

Through years of coaching and interacting with many people, I've observed a recurring pattern. Besides those who've already achieved their desired success and are living purposefully, there seem to be two distinct groups, or stages of people who are aspiring and desiring to do so. Interestingly, I've personally had the opportunity to experience both of these stages. One group are those who are just getting started, stepping out, toe dipping, and exploring alternatives to mainstream lifestyle - recognizing there must be more to life than living "ordinarily" and are keen to discover more. The other group are those who are already involved in the personal development space and are learning and growing personally and spiritually, but have not yet achieved the success and breakthroughs they desire. Many in this group have spent lots of time and money reading books, attending seminars, and studying courses and programmes. However, they are still struggling in some areas and not living in full alignment with their purpose, or they are not yet experiencing the successful results they believe they are meant to have.

This book is intended as a companion and guide for those who, like me, have always felt a deep curiosity and an inner knowing that there must be more to our lives than simply existing. The idea of living a purely physical life, devoid of any real purpose, followed by an inevitable end, has never resonated with me. This yearning for something beyond the ordinary has led me to explore alternative paths, and it is this exploration that I share with you on these pages. I also spent years trying to figure out my purpose and how to live a successful and purposeful life, including many of my earlier years in a religious missionary cult. Then, in more recent years, I have invested my time and money in studying, and experiencing as many different self-development and spiritually aligned courses, and programmes as I could get my hands on. There's a lot of good material out there these days, but we can easily get caught up in new marketing offers - that new free e-book, that discounted study course or special book offer, and not really focus on applying and living the advice given. I believe this is the main cause of people getting discouraged and disillusioned with themselves, feeling they just can't "make this stuff work" in their own lives. There are common threads that run through all of the legitimate materials, from the oldest manuscripts of the ancient sages to the latest social media posts and courses from today's enlightened mystics and channels of light. You can take any one of hundreds, or even thousands, of different legitimate teachers, organizations and teachings out there these days and apply their teachings in your life and make it work if you make a committed decision to do so and then stay with it until it happens. If a particular person or teaching or concept doesn't resonate with you, then you can choose to simply scroll on past until you find what does. I've noticed that there are some people who like to deep dive into following one person, or one organization's teachings and techniques - sticking with one tribe. Whereas others prefer plenty of variety in what they read and listen and who they interact with. And that's perfectly fine. The key here is not who you follow or what modality you choose, but that you make use of the best resources you can find and commit to doing the inner work of growing and becoming the best version of yourself. And only you can do that.

    This book is your guide to discovering your life's true purpose, by helping peel back the layers of environmental and societal programming, that we have all, both consciously and unconsciously adopted so that you can uncover the treasure trove of your authentic self. Within each of us lies a unique blueprint, a divine spark waiting to be fully ignited. We each have a role to play in our movie on centre stage. And our role is not to be a part of a general crowd scene or even a supporting actor. You are the producer, the director, and the star – the main character in your life's movie. Your job is to figure out who you are meant to be and then put yourself out there and become it – to play your role fully and unapologetically! My wish for you is eloquently captured by Wayne Dyer in his famous words: *"Don't die with the music still in you."*

Discovering and living your purpose is like being guided by your north star - a trusted compass for your life, based on your deepest values, desires, and convictions. It's being led by your heart and not by the ever-changing physical world around us.

Gone are the days of placing blind faith in external deities or religions. True faith and trust that can empower us for any challenges that come our way is found within - in embracing the awareness of our Life Force Energy – that same Energy that beats our hearts, makes the flower grow, and keeps the planets on course. We are each a magnificent, unique embodiment of Divine Love emanating from this Energy Source. Know that you can safely believe and trust in your life's purpose and mission in life, as it is connected with this Life Force Energy within us. Dear Gabby Bernstein's book title says it so well *"The Universe has Your Back."*

As you discover and live your life's purpose, keep in mind that it is not set in stone, and you will probably find yourself fine-tuning it and iterating it often as you step into becoming all that you are meant to be. Sometimes, you'll feel right on purpose, while other times, you'll feel like you're wading through deep waters of uncertainty and confusion. It's like two of Tony Robbin's six basic needs for humanity; one of them is certainty and security, and another one is uncertainty, change, and variety. *Knowing* our life's purpose can provide safety and security. *Living* it can provide uncertainty, change, and variety. Enjoy the dance!

What Does "Life's Purpose" Mean?

Purpose is Spirit seeking expression - **Kevin Cashman.**

Our life's purpose is the core reason for our existence. It asks those scary questions of "Who am I?" and "Why have I shown up on this planet?" Part of what makes it seem so difficult to address is that it is not measurable or quantifiable by our five senses. It's intangible, and there's no right or wrong, black-or-white answer to the question of "What is your life's purpose?" and that gets uncomfortable for many people, especially those who tend to like things to be all figured out logically and filed away in measurable compartments.

Our life's purpose is that underlying impetus or power that silently guides us and influences our thoughts, feelings, behaviours, decisions, and actions. Sometimes, it's stifled or hindered or even blocked, and at other times, it is burning brightly in our lives. It often reveals itself through our energy levels and our emotions and feelings, as well as our thoughts and responses. Sometimes, it is through our intuition, our heart and gut reactions, and our bodily sensations.

Our true life's purpose is not subject to the many changing circumstances of the physical world we live in. It stands firm regardless of what we encounter in this world of changing environments, people, circumstances, and conditions. That's the beauty of discovering it, as it can be used as a ballast and firm foundation, a "true north" that we can anchor to as we navigate our way through life's often unpredictable journey.

Our life's purpose runs deeper than our short-term plans and the goals and visions we may have for our lives. It is more than our personality, likes and dislikes, or even our passions and preferences – although all of these can be clues to discovering and understanding our purpose, as you will see in later chapters. Our life's purpose can be realized in many different circumstances and is not usually dependent on a specific lifestyle or even specific people in our lives. As you refine your life's purpose through the guidance in this book, you will discover that it is very adaptable and not dependent on a certain set of outer physical circumstances. It runs silently from within at the soul level.

It's exciting to discover your life's purpose. It's exciting to feel that you're in alignment and on track. You're doing what you're meant to do and being who you're meant to be. Discovering your life's purpose is rooted in the understanding that you are a spiritual being having a human experience. Before you were born, you may have chosen this journey and, being aware of its challenges and rewards and final outcomes, said, "Yes, I'm up for it!" All the philosophical and spiritual traditions talk about your soul and your spirit coming into your body for a purpose, and then, once the purpose is fulfilled, it transitions and leaves your body. We have all arrived here with a return ticket. And there's a purpose for it all. It doesn't matter how you think you arrived on this planet – whether you've got a religious connotation to it, or it's the next unfoldment or incarnation of your life, or you were a newly created soul, or something else - each of us has special coding that is uniquely imprinted within our DNA. Just like an acorn seed that grows into an oak tree, it has a unique type of branch, leaf, size, and shape determined by everything contained in that seed. It's already encoded in the seed before it even gets started. And it's the same with us. We are each uniquely imprinted and hardwired. We don't just go through life randomly, living by chance; we discover our purpose and what we're good at because we're meant to discover it, just as we're meant to figure out what our legs do and how our fingers work. Our unique imprints are hardwired into our system just as surely as our lungs are given their blueprint to breathe. And it's from this coding of specific traits and proclivities, talents and gifts, desires and values that we're able to discover and live our life's purpose.

One way to understand and visualize our life's purpose is to see it from what is sometimes called the "God's eye view" - the perspective of an observer looking at something from above or from the future. For example, you can look at a caterpillar and see that humble caterpillar crawling around in the dirt. Then, it goes into a cocoon and later emerges as a beautiful butterfly with rainbow wings. You see it flying amongst the flowers, bringing joy to a little child and a smile to an elderly person marvelling at its beauty. That caterpillar does not just exist randomly. It's on purpose. Likewise, seeing our life's purpose with the "God's eye view" will help us better understand its significance.

Why Does it Matter?

Musicians must make music, artists must paint, poets must write if they are to ultimately be at peace with themselves. What human beings can be, they must be – **Abraham Maslow.**

In life, some may feel content to drift aimlessly, swept along by the currents of circumstance without much concern for where they're headed. They live reactively, accepting whatever comes their way as inevitable, believing they have no control over the unfolding of their lives. If that's your perspective, then perhaps pondering your life's purpose may seem irrelevant. But I would say that type of person, or a person with that type of perception of life, is in the minority. Most of us, including you if you've picked up this book, care deeply about our lives, about humanity, and the world we live in. We seek meaning and direction, striving to understand our purpose on this planet in order to live our lives to the fullest.

For some people, their purpose in life is very clear - they just know they're destined to be a musician, for example. They write music every day, and they've been doing it since grade school. They're good at it, totally fulfilled, and happy doing it until the day they die. That's obviously their calling, their purpose, and that's what they love to do. However, for the majority of us, it isn't quite as clear as that. We may know that we want to "play our music", and confidently do what we are good at, and excel in areas that bring us joy and fulfillment. And knowing that is certainly a good first step. As you allow yourself to be open and receptive while reading through these pages, it is my hope that some exciting new insights and discoveries will emerge that will enlighten your path ahead.

Without a sense of purpose, our lives can become a chaotic game of chance. We may stumble through relationships, health crises, financial struggles, and emotional and lifestyle challenges - never quite sure of our footing. We can be forever "throwing mud at the wall to see what sticks". Fear, doubt, and anxiety can cloud our days, casting shadows over our potential for growth and happiness. But it doesn't have to be that way. There are clues and cues and signs happening around us all the time. The Universe, God, Life Force Energy, or whatever term you use, is always gently guiding us and helping us understand ourselves and our purpose in life. You don't need to be a mystical guru, or a shaman to figure it out. It can be quite basic and simple, although it may also be emotional or intuitive guidance that is being sensed. It may be something new and different that we've got to try and wrap our finite, five sensory brains around it in order to express it or explain it. But as long as we're seeking and asking and listening and keeping an open mind, we'll see the signs and discover our unique path. It'll appear. As someone wisely said, "What you are seeking is seeking you."

Trusting in Your Life's Purpose

The two most important days in life are the day you were born and the day you find out why – **Mark Twain.**

As you refine your life's purpose, you'll notice your life starts to become more anchored and grounded. Your purpose becomes a solid foundation you can depend on and place your full trust and faith in. Your life is no longer adrift. As the famous old Biblical story says, *"A wise man builds his house on the rock, and a foolish man builds his house on the sand."* Once you align yourself with your purpose and mission, you are no longer affected or tossed around so much. You no longer feel the need to react to all the drama going on, whether it be with people and relationships, or money and careers, or health and lifestyle, or whatever. Everything in the outside world around you is always constantly changing. As the Greek philosopher Heraclitus said, *"You can never step in the same river twice, for it's not the same river and you're not the same person."*

Amidst life's sometimes wild and unpredictable journey—with its ups, downs, and unexpected twists and turns—your purpose can act as a guiding light, a true north for your soul. It can provide stability amidst chaos, a sanctuary to return to when the storms of life batter you and you don't know where to turn. This trust in your purpose isn't a mere belief; it's a profound inner knowing akin to the faith some people place in a religion. Yet, unlike external deities and traditional religions, your life's purpose is deeply personal and intrinsic, residing within the core of your being. It's who you are!

In my life, a clear understanding of my purpose has proven to be an invaluable resource. It acts as a powerful force, propelling me forward even when faced with seemingly insurmountable challenges or emotionally draining situations. In those moments, taking a conscious pause to step back and realign with my core purpose allows me to detach from drama, whether physical or mental and find a sense of calm. This shift in perspective allows me to realize that these fleeting circumstances hold little sway over my deeper purpose-driven existence. It's such a relief to know that, "Yes, I am doing fine. I'm still aligned with my life's purpose and that these external challenges are going to sort themselves out. I know what I'm here for. The darkness may seem overwhelming now, but like any storm, it will pass. Soon, I will see clearly again, ready to take the next steps on my path and journey in life."

People put their faith and trust in all kinds of things – religions, gurus, mentors, metaphysical events, family, careers, businesses, and even possessions. But at the end of the day, no one and certainly nothing on the outside is coming to save you. You can only get that inner strength and assurance from within; nothing on the external can give you that. True power lies in recognizing your infinite potential and trusting your life's purpose. This is an inside job – it's an inner knowing, a powerful alignment with the essence of your being, a connection to your intrinsic power and energy. Embracing your life's purpose is aligning with the very essence of life itself. It's your power source.

Clues to Discovering Your Life's Purpose

The whole secret of a successful life is to find out what is one's destiny to do, and then do it - **Henry Ford.**

Let's look at some different ideas and ways that you can discover your life's purpose. Remember, it is not a one-time event; it's an ongoing journey of self-discovery and refinement. I've refined the wording and structure of my life's purpose many times as I have come to understand it more. Just like a computer app, it may start with version 1.0 and then upgrades to version 1.2, then 2.0, and so on. Earl Nightingale's definition of success serves as a good illustration here *"Success is the progressive realization of a worthy ideal"* I personally like to keep my life's purpose defined as simply as possible, just one or two sentences rather than a lengthy explanation. It might start as a long explanation or maybe even a "brain dump" of everything you can think of that matters to you, and then refine it, trim it down, and tweak it to what succinctly fits. Here are some clues that you may find helpful in discovering your purpose, or if you have already discovered it, you may find it helpful in refining it further.

Core Values and Beliefs

Open your arms to change but don't let go of your values

– Dalai Lama.

Your core values serve as the compass guiding you on your life's journey. They resonate deep within you, shaping your beliefs and decisions. One of the easiest ways of understanding and recognizing your core values is to simply look over a list of values and notice which ones stand out and resonate with you - which one's matter to you the most. I have included an extensive list of values on the next pages that should give you some ideas of where your true values lie. Take a look and pick out three or four - or five or six, that are important and that matter to you. Or if it is difficult to narrow it down to that few, go ahead and select 12 or 15, or even 20. Once you have those pulled out, then narrow it down further to an ideal amount of 3-5 core values. Your core values are what you recognize as most important to you. They are the things you notice yourself talking about often. They are what you find yourself naturally arguing for if there's a discussion going on. Or maybe they're those silent values that you allow to guide you quietly in your decisions, conversations, and choices. You'll know which ones they are - and if you are uncertain of one, it's probably not a core value.

Your core values are key clues to discovering and aligning with your purpose. Core values are a part of your DNA and your soul being. They're not just a part of some new belief or fad you try for a while and then drop. They're a part of you and unique to you. You can probably look back on your life and see where these values have shaped your perspectives, your point of view on something, your priorities, and your decision-making. What you value is what you allow to guide you and shape your life, your beliefs, and the way you interpret things.

It's crucial here to discern the difference between core values and those values adopted from external influences. Be sure you are aligning with your true core values and not some "well-meaning" values that you have accepted as being a part of your life and make-up. These "well-meaning" values could have been picked up from your parents or friends or your workplace or surroundings. They could be values you think other people would like about you, or values you think you should emulate because it's the "expected" way to be. As you take an honest look, listen to your heart, and assess what really matters to you. You'll know.

List of Values

Abundance	Calmness
Acceptance	Carefulness/Cautious
Accomplishment/ Achievement	Caring
	Certainty
Accountability	Challenge
Accuracy	Change/Variety
Adaptability	Charisma
Adventure	Charity
Affection	Children/Parenting
Altruism	Clarity
Ambition	Cleanliness
Appreciation	Comfort
Ascension	Commitment
Authenticity	Common sense
Authority	Communication
Awareness/ Consciousness	Community
	Compassion
Balance	Competence/Capable
Beauty	Concentration
Being Present	Confidence
Being Realistic	Connection with a Higher Power
Being Selfless	
Being the best	Consistency
Belonging	Contemplation/ Mindfulness/ Reflection
Bliss/Awe/Wonder	
Boldness	
Bravery	Contentment

Peter Wescombe

Contribution	Entrepreneurialism
Control	Planet/Environment
Conviction	Equality
Cooperation	Ethics
Courage	Excellence/Mastery
Courtesy	Excitement
Creativity	Experience
Credibility	Exploration
Curiosity	Expression
Decisiveness	Facilitation
Dedication	Fairness
Dependability	Faith
Determination	Fame
Devotion	Family
Dignity	Fearlessness
Discipline	Feeling Safe and Secure
Discovery	
Diversity	Feelings and Emotions
Drive	
Ease and Flow	Feminine Energy
Effectiveness	Fidelity
Efficiency	Financial Stability
Empathy	Finesse
Empowerment	Fitness
Encouragement	Focus
Endurance	Foresight
Energy	Forgiveness
Enjoyment	Fortitude
Entertainment	Freedom
Enthusiasm	Friendships

Fulfillment/Satisfaction	Improvement
Fun	Inclusion
Future generations	Independence/Autonomy
Generosity	Individuality
Genius	Influence
Giving	Initiative
Giving People a Chance	Inner Guidance
	Inner Peace
God/Higher Power/The Universe	Innovation
	Insightful
Goodness	Inspiration
Grace	Integrity
Gratitude	Intelligence
Greatness	Intensity
Growth/Expansion/Fuller Expression	Intention
	Intuition
Happiness	Joy
Hard work	Justice
Harmony	Kindness
Health	Knowledge
Holistic Living	Lawfulness
Home	Leadership
Honesty	Learning
Honor	Legacy
Hope	Leisure
Humanity	Letting go/Detachment
Humility	
Humour	Love
Imagination	Love of Career

Loyalty	Productivity
Making a difference	Professionalism
Masculine energy	Purpose/Mission/ Dharma
Mind control	
Moderation	Quality
Motivation	Reason and Logic
Nature	Recognition
Non-duality/ Oneness/Unity	Recreation
	Relationships
Nutrition	Reliability
Openness	Religions
Optimism	Reputation
Order/Organization	Resourcefulness
Originality/ Uniqueness	Respect
	Responsibility
Parenting	Results-oriented
Passion	Reverence
Patience	Risk-taking
Patriotism	Self-discipline
Peace	Self-expression
Perception	Self-love and Self-care
Performance	Self-reliance
Perseverance	Self-respect
Persistence	Sensitivity
Personal Development	Sensuousness
Personal Empowerment	Serenity
	Service/Philanthropy
Personal Fulfillment	Sharing
Playfulness	Significance
Pleasure	Silence

Simplicity	Wealth and Prosperity
Sincerity	Wellness/Well-being
Skilfulness	Wholeheartedness
Solitude	Willingness
Spirituality	Winning
Spontaneity	Wisdom
Stability	Working smarter - not Harder.
Status	
Stewardship	
Success	
Sustainability	
Teamwork/Collaboration	
Thankfulness/Gratitude	
Letting Go/Detachment	
Time	
Tolerance	
Tranquillity/Equanimity	
Transparency/Openness	
Travel/Exploring	
Trust in a Higher Power	
Trustworthiness	
Truth	
Vision	
Vulnerability	

Passions, Desires, and Ambitions

If you can't figure out your purpose, figure out your passion. For your passion will lead you right into your purpose."
— **Bishop T.D. Jakes**

What are you passionate about? What are you obsessed with? What do you have a burning desire to do, be, or have? Your passions and desires unveil glimpses of your purpose. Things that come to mind may be physical - like being in nature or gardening. You might be passionate about making music or other creative arts. It could be a love for intricate details or engineering or tinkering with car engines. It could be playing a sport. As you look at your passions and desires, look a little deeper and notice what is causing you to have that passion and desire. For example, maybe you're passionate about riding motorcycles, or you have an ambition to own a yacht and sail out in the open seas. As you look deeper, you may discover that your core values are freedom and adventure. In this example, riding a motorbike or being in a yacht on the ocean is not necessarily your purpose in life. They're more like visions and goals of things that you enjoy because they make you feel good and alive. They make you feel aligned with a part of your life's purpose for freedom and adventure. While some of these pursuits that you are passionate about may not be your specific life's purpose, they offer clues to understanding and aligning with your deeper calling.

Think about activities and projects that excite you. What lights you up and gets you excited? What do you love talking about? What do you like to be a part of? It could be a noble aspiration like solving global hunger or helping humanity to be more united and put an end to war and violence. It could also be in a more personal area, like creating a close family legacy, establishing a beautiful home and property, being a world traveller, or having a wonderful relationship. It could also be service or benevolence oriented, such as creating facilities for health and wellness in a natural setting. Take some time to listen to your heart and ask yourself: What do I really want? What do I truly desire in my heart of hearts? Are there some secret wants, desires, and ambitions that I haven't really expressed? What am I passionate about? If money or time or people's opinions didn't matter, what would I do? What do I love to read and research or talk about in conversations with friends and loved ones? What do I find myself daydreaming about? Those are all noteworthy clues. Recall a time when you were in love with someone; you didn't need to write out affirmations reminding yourself, "I must think about this person", or "I need to love this person." No! The person you were in love with showed up like a huge hologram in front of you wherever you went. You couldn't stop thinking about them. That's how it is with your true desires and ambitions once you clear away the clutter and busyness of life and start to embrace them. They're a part of you – they're already there. You don't have to create, make them up, or pretend anything.

Interests and Curiosity

Once we believe in ourselves, we can risk curiosity, wonder, spontaneous delight, or any experience that reveals the human spirit
- **E. E. Cummings.**

What captures your interest? What arouses your curiosity? Pay attention to what draws you, what appeals to you, and what piques your interest because that's where your energy naturally flows. Like the famous quote, *"Energy flows where your attention goes."* Your interests reflect what matters to you, so take note of where your attention goes. Allow yourself to explore those areas further without feeling restricted or restrained by societal norms or the expectations and opinions of others. Break free and get out of your comfort zone. Stretch, expand, and explore new things, as well as venture into new and different playing fields. Don't worry about yourself thinking that you are giving yourself false hopes, or you are being unrealistic and that "it will never happen to me." I agree with Michelangelo when he said, *"The greatest danger for most of us is not that our aim is too high and we miss it, but that we aim too low, and we reach it."* We too easily allow ourselves to settle, and live lives of mediocrity instead of "letting go of the reigns" of our interest and curiosity and seeing where it takes us. Explore your interests and whatever sparks your curiosity, even if they lead you down unconventional or non-mainstream paths. You might discover that all this time, you have been a square peg trying to be fitted into a round hole.

Listening to Your Heart and Connecting to Source Energy

> *Follow your heart and your intuition. They somehow already know what you truly want to become. Everything else is secondary* - **Steve Jobs.**

These days, practices like meditation, mindfulness, intuitive listening, and other modalities that connect us with our Source of Energy are accepted as legitimate. People recognize the importance of spending time in stillness and maintaining an inner connection and alignment amidst the chaos of life in the fast lanes of today. These practices enable us to tap into our higher awareness and provide portals for empowerment and elevating our energy levels. They are essential tools for grounding and distancing ourselves from the endless chatter that goes on in our minds so much of the time. By engaging in these modalities, we open ourselves up to receiving guidance and insights that align with our true purpose.

There's no one-size-fits-all approach to spiritual and soulful connection. How you connect and what you want to call "It" is a personal matter. Just do what works for you, and in the way you feel most comfortable and authentic with. Whether you choose to call "it" your Higher self, God, Life force energy, the Universe, Awareness, Consciousness, Nature, the Dao, Spirit, or a million other names that can be used, it doesn't matter. Likewise, whether you use meditation, chanting, sound healing, prayer, mindfulness, silence, hypnosis, singing, dancing, walking in nature, hugging trees, or any other way to connect, it also doesn't matter. You can get all the advice and opinions you want, but when all is said and done, you are the only one responsible for your life, so do what works for you. If you don't already know what works best for you, or if you haven't connected in a way you feel comfortable with yet, try experimenting with different techniques and portals and/or find someone who can help guide you in getting connected on a deeper soul level. *(or feel free to reach out to us via the email address given at the beginning of the book)* There's nothing to be afraid of in exploring the spiritual, non-physical realms, despite all the old-school religious superstitions and stories about evil and demons coming to scare you if you dare go there and venture into the unseen world of spirit. Embrace the diversity of spiritual and metaphysical practices freely and allow them to guide you on your journey towards discovering your life's purpose.

Living in the Moment

> *Life is only available in the here and now. The past is already gone, and the future is yet to come...there is only one moment for me to live...The present moment* - **Thich Nhat Hanh**

All the great masters have emphasized that the only time we have is now – this present moment. As Wayne Dyer explained, our past is like the wake, or the wave of foam, a boat generates as it moves through the water. You look back, and you see the foam trail that's left behind as the boat travels through the water. The wake doesn't drive the boat or have any impact on the direction of the boat. It's just the trail that's left behind. And he's right; we need to see our past simply as the trail that's left behind and not allow it to have any power or control our lives today with its baggage of limited mindsets or its inventory of all our failures and shortcomings that it is constantly trying to impose upon us.

And the future doesn't exist. It is simply an illusion of possibilities constructed by our minds. The present moment is all we have to work with – it's where life unfolds, where possibilities and opportunities and creativeness dwells.

As you step back and reflect and be mindful of this present moment, you realize that there are limitless possibilities available - absolutely anything is possible. Take a minute or two right now to consciously release and let go of all your thoughts – any negative thoughts and concerns about the past, as well as any anxious and apprehensive thoughts about the future. Simply breathe and embrace the present moment. As you do this, contemplate your ideal life and its purpose and notice what emerges. It may offer valuable insights into your true calling. Doing this often can be a simple, easy, and non-time-consuming way of connecting with your Higher Self and getting clarity on your purpose – a basic form of meditation and mindfulness.

> *"What day is it?" asked Pooh*
> *"It's today," squeaked Piglet*
> *"My favourite day," said Pooh*
> **- A.A. Milne**

Moments of Flow and Fulfillment.

Going with the flow is responding to cues from the Universe. When you go with the flow, you're surfing life force. It's about wakeful trust and total collaboration with what's showing up for you
- **Danielle LaPorte.**

Have you ever found yourself swept away by a current of inspiring thoughts, ideas, and sensations? It's like your mind takes off on a journey of its own, exploring new territories beyond the mundane routines of everyday life. Maybe it happens after a moment of mindfulness, a walk in nature, or even when you're having a shower. It could be a thought implanted by what someone said, that you begin contemplating, or something that momentarily caught your attention in a social media feed that triggered further reflection. Or it can be a brand-new creative idea bubbling up from your intuition or imagination faculties. Regardless of how it was triggered, your mind picked up on it, and your thoughts and feelings are off and running with it. Pay attention to what captures your attention and sets off your imagination - and where it takes you. Nothing is random – it's all a part of your life's unfoldment.

What Energizes You, and What Drains You?

Sometimes letting things go is an act of far greater power than defending or hanging on - **Eckhart Tolle.**

Notice what fuels your energy and what depletes it. Take stock of your feelings, not just your emotions but also the sensations in your body, the subtle signals from your nervous system. Those moments of uneasiness or anxiety can be like signals or pointers, trying to nudge you away from what's not aligned with you. Whereas those sparks of empowerment, those little "aha" moments leave you feeling invigorated and thinking, "Hey, wouldn't that be fun to try?" That's your soul aligning with that frequency and guiding you in the direction of your purpose.

Your interactions with people and the circumstances around you also carry clues. Pay attention to how certain individuals or situations make you feel. Some might leave you feeling drained, while others uplift and inspire you. Take time to reflect and consider who they are and what they are doing. These can be clues. Notice who and what's resonating with you in an empowering way.

Life has a way of sending signs, coincidences, and serendipitous encounters that seem tailor-made for you. Embrace these moments of synchronicity, where the universe seems to be arranging the people and/or events that are coming your way. Open yourself to vulnerability, allowing these experiences to influence and shape your journey. Be an active participant in your dance of life. Run with the thoughts that light you up, the people who lift you higher, and the circumstances that spark joy within you. This is your path to living a life of purpose and fulfillment.

Milestones, Patterns and Pivotal Moments

You can't connect the dots looking forward; you can only connect them looking backwards. So, you have to trust that the dots will somehow connect in your future. You have to trust in something - your gut, destiny, life, karma, whatever -
Steve Jobs.

As we embark on the journey of uncovering our life's purpose, one invaluable clue lies in the tapestry of our past experiences. Take a moment to reflect on the pivotal moments that have shaped your journey thus far. Consider the times when you felt truly alive when your soul seemed to dance in pure joy and bliss. These moments could be anything - a surprising success, a daunting challenge you overcame, or even a simple act that exceeded your expectations. Whatever emerges as you reflect on this, obviously left an indelible impression, which is why it has come to mind now. Pay attention to these past experiences as you are being reminded of some of your inherent potential, some unique gifts you possess, and glimpses of your authentic self, all of which can be clues to your life's purpose.

Similarly, ponder upon those moments where you faltered or felt out of place. Perhaps you found yourself in situations that didn't align with your true nature, where you felt awkward and uncomfortable or out of place. These moments, too, hold valuable insights, guiding us away from non-aligned experiences and towards activities and paths that resonate with us in positive, feel-good ways.

Hobbies, Free-time Activities, and Volunteer Projects

> *Successful technologies often begin as hobbies. Jacques Cousteau invented scuba diving because he enjoyed exploring caves. The Wright brothers invented flying as a relief from the monotony of their normal business of selling and repairing bicycles.*
>
> **– Freeman Dyson**

In observing our free time pursuits and hobbies, we can catch a glimpse of our intrinsic passions and inclinations. What activities do you find yourself naturally drawn to when you have a bit of extra time? What do you enjoy doing for fun and pleasure? Whether it's tinkering with hobbies or immersing yourself in creative projects, these endeavours can often provide clues to "connecting the dots" to your purpose driven future. Notice what you have often engaged in in the past, and even now, during your leisure time?

Consider also the acts of service and volunteerism that you like to engage in. What do you enjoy doing for others - whether you get paid for it or not? There is a profound joy in giving of oneself, in extending a helping hand to others without expectation. Whether it's baking cupcakes for some friends and loved ones, or simply sharing a cup of tea, these acts of kindness speak volumes about our inherent desire to uplift and connect with those around us.

What I've discovered in my own life, and in talking with many people about their life's purpose, is that it is often related to service or helping humanity in some way, either directly or indirectly. Wayne Dyer wisely reminds us to ask ourselves, *"Who may I serve?"* and *"How may I serve?"* Keep an open heart and a willingness to explore this. Your life's purpose may very well be intertwined with acts of service and kindness and linked with a deep desire to be a beneficial presence for humanity. It was Mahatma Gandhi who profoundly said, *"The best way to find yourself is to lose yourself in the service of others."*

What do Your Friends and Family Say About You?

> *Surround yourself with good people. People who are going to be honest with you and look out for your best interests*
> **- Derek Jeter**

Have you ever stopped to listen to what your friends, family, and others say about you? It can be like having a mirror reflecting parts of yourself you might not have noticed. Paying attention to these reflections can help guide you towards uncovering your life's purpose. Maybe someone mentions how you always lift their spirits or spark creativity around them. Or maybe your partner will say, "You're always in the garage, tinkering around, building, or inventing or fixing things for other people." What are people saying about you? These observations, whether positive, or areas for growth, offer valuable clues about your purpose.

Natural Gifts, Talents, and Abilities

Hide not your talents. They for use were made. What's a sundial in the shade? - **Benjamin Franklin**

Our natural talents and abilities, that we seem to be born with, are often intricately woven into our life's purpose. Some people recognize their talents early on, especially those inclined towards creativity in music, arts, or invention. While with others, these gifts can remain dormant, waiting for the right moment to reveal themselves. You might have spent years in a profession that didn't align with your true talents. Maybe you have been an accountant for years while harbouring a passion for writing. Then, one day, you take a leap and start writing. The words flow effortlessly, captivating you in a way you never expected. It dawns on you: "Wow, I not only love this, but I'm actually good at it!" At that moment, you've just uncovered one of your innate abilities, a spark that could illuminate your life's purpose.

Operating in the area(s) of natural abilities tends to generate joy and pleasure and ease and flow and a feeling of purpose and fulfillment, as compared with the need to grind it out and work long and hard that is often associated with learning new skills that don't come so naturally, or doing work that always feels like hard work. Doing what you love and are naturally good at, always trumps training and learning skills that were imposed on you.

Peter Wescombe

Allow Yourself to Dream and Imagine

Imagination is more important than knowledge. For knowledge is limited to all we now know and understand, while imagination embraces the entire world — **Albert Einstein.**

Everything that now exists was created twice – once in our imagination and once in the physical world. Our imagination is an amazing mental faculty that, unfortunately, gets stifled and cast aside very early in life. Take a moment to reminisce about your childhood dreams and fantasies. Maybe if you're a guy, you always wanted to be a fireman, or if you're a girl, you wanted to be a ballerina or a Barbie girl? While they may seem a bit far-fetched or immature now, some childhood dreams can hold clues to your deeper desires and inclinations. Delve deeper into the symbolism behind those dreams and fantasies. Perhaps there's a thread connecting them to your present-day aspirations.

Embrace the playful, curious spirit of your inner child. Engage in imaginative exploration, allowing yourself to discover new facets of your true self. Rediscover the joy of playfulness and light-heartedness. Let go of convention and logic and see where it takes you. Ask yourself some new creative questions like "I wonder what it would be like to try this," "What are some different ways to get better results here?" and "What if this does work?" History shows us that most of the groundbreaking inventions and discoveries we have today stemmed from "normal" people who dared to dream and imagine different realities. Thomas Edison dreamed of illuminating the world and imagined an idea of how it could be done. The Wright Brothers were ridiculed for dreaming and imagining people flying in contraptions through the air. Thank God they did act on and follow their dreams. As you give yourself permission to dream and venture into the realm of your imagination, you can tap into a wellspring of creativity and innovative ideas that can ignite your passion and reveal your purpose.

Experimenting with Different Paths and Activities

Negative results are just what I want. They're just as valuable to me as positive results. I can never find the thing that does the job best until I find the ones that don't - **Thomas A. Edison.**

In the journey of life, there are moments when we feel a bit stuck and uncertain about which direction to take. It's during these times that experimenting with different paths and activities can offer profound insights. As the old saying goes, *"The boat has to be in motion before the rudder can take effect."* Sometimes, stepping out and trying different things, as well as embracing a mindset of curiosity and exploration, is what is required. You don't need to commit fully right away; just dip your toes in, test the waters, and see what resonates with your soul. Dabbling here and there, chatting with people about new ideas, and just seeing where you go with it can be very helpful.

Of course, don't invest too deeply in something initially if it doesn't feel right, or if it starts imposing a significant financial burden. Recognize when to pivot. If a pursuit becomes overly challenging or consistently draining, it may not align with your true purpose. Grant yourself the freedom to reassess and change course as needed. But, if you glimpse a shimmering possibility on the horizon, despite the hurdles along the way, summon the courage to persevere.

A seeming failure or defeat, or recognizing your actions are not bringing the results you intended, gives you some contrast and clarity on your path's direction. Like Price Pritchett said, *"a rocket "fails" its way to the moon by continually making mistakes and self-correcting them in order to stay on course."*

Life is a grand experiment, a playground for exploration and growth. Even during challenging times, embrace the spirit of playfulness. Allow yourself to navigate through the twists and turns, discovering new facets of yourself and the world around you. By remaining open to the adventure, you will uncover hidden treasures and unexpected blessings along the way that illuminate your path to uncovering and fulfilling your life's work.

Hindrances and Blocks to Discovering Your Life's Purpose

Life is what happens to you while you're busy making other plans — **John Lennon.**

There are always plenty of reasons and excuses why you are not able to discover your life's purpose, or why you would even want to. We think, "There's just so much to do in life, so many things to keep us busy, who's got time to find out what our life's purpose is," which is a pretty insane way of thinking. It's the "hamster wheel" mentality — there's too much going on to stop for a minute and take a look at where we're headed. Let's delve into some of the common hindrances that can deter us from embarking on this path.

Negative Religious Connotations with Life's Purpose

As a spiritual being, you fear nothing because you know there is nothing to fear, and all that truly exists in the world is love
- Deepak Chopra.

Discovering our life's purpose shouldn't be hampered by religious dogma or societal norms. Unfortunately, because of past conditioning from parents, institutions, social pressure, societal customs, etc., people often equate discovering life's purposes with following a religion or some spiritual path. However, it's a deeply personal journey, unique to each individual, and no one is obligated to pay homage to external Gods or deities in order to explore and discover their purpose in life. It can be connected to religion if that's what you want, or it can totally not be. It's personal and unique to you, and whether you use a religious or metaphysical viewpoint, an atheistic or scientific perspective, or none of the above to discover it, it totally depends on how you feel led and guided. Don't allow religion or religious dogma to block you or hinder you from discovering your life's purpose. As we covered in one of the previous sections, there's nothing to be afraid of despite all the old-school religious superstitions and stories about evil and demons coming to scare you if you dare go there. Feel free to embrace the diversity of spiritual and metaphysical practices and allow them to guide you on your journey towards discovering your life's purpose.

Mindsets and Limiting Beliefs

Everything depends on your self-concept —and your concept of yourself is all that you accept and consent to as true about yourself. That which you will not affirm to be true about yourself can never be realized by you. — **Neville Goddard.**

The beliefs and the concepts we have of ourselves shape our outside physical reality. Many of us harbor limiting beliefs and scarcity mindsets that keep us locked into living lives of mediocrity, holding us back from realizing our full potential. These beliefs and habitual ways of living - often ingrained since childhood and influenced by our environment, act like internal thermostats, keeping us living and operating within our "safe" comfort zones. But just as a thermostat can be adjusted, so too can our mindsets and limitations. It starts with recognizing what you honestly believe about yourself — your self-concept or self-image, and what you believe you are capable of. This recognition, or self-awareness is the starting point for conscious change. There are many wonderful ways to shift and change the images and concepts we have of ourselves and break free from habits of limitation and mediocrity. Addressing them here is beyond the scope of this book, although we will touch on it a little in later chapters. For now, just be aware that recognizing and pursuing your true purpose may mean stretching and getting out from under those self-made limitations and giving yourself a fresh, clean slate — a new perspective, to work from. As Les Brown wisely stated, *"Life has no limitations, except the ones you make."*

Arguing for Your Limitations

Argue for your limitations, and sure enough, they're yours
— **Richard Bach.**

Too often, we find ourselves defending our limitations instead of embracing our possibilities. Someone can present a new idea or a new possibility to us and we habitually find ourselves arguing for why it can't be done, or arguing for staying the way we are - creating a case for why we can't do it – often with the classic response of, "But you don't understand." This type of response can usually be summed up in one word: "excuses." Excuses become a shield against change, a way to justify staying stagnant. It's very easy to make legitimate and logical excuses why we shouldn't do something. But what if we challenged these excuses? What if we dared to entertain the idea of stepping into the unknown? What if instead we asked ourselves some empowering questions, like "I wonder how I could make that idea work?" or like Tim Ferris's radical questioning, *"What would this look like if it were easy?"* Instead of arguing for our limitations, let's open ourselves to accepting new perspectives and limitless opportunities so we can explore the full spectrum of our life's purpose possibilities.

Peter Wescombe

Fear of the Unknown, and Autonomic Nervous System Responses.

Big ships might look impressive sitting in the harbour, but that is not what they were built for - **Unknown.**

One of our autonomic nervous systems primary functions is to ensure our safety and well-being by maintaining a sense of predictability and routine. It's wired to resist change and avoid risks, keeping us within our comfort zone where everything feels familiar and secure. When we entertain thoughts of stepping outside this comfort zone, whether it's trying something new or exploring new possibilities, our body and mind instinctively recoils. We're sometimes flooded with feelings of fear and apprehension, warning us against venturing into the unknown. This resistance to change is deeply ingrained in our psyche, often rooted in past experiences and familiar patterns of behaviour. It's the voice of our past, echoing the familiar refrain of sticking to what we know and avoiding the unfamiliar. However, this inclination to stay within our comfort zone acts as a barrier to growth and exploration. Breaking free from this cycle requires courage and a willingness to challenge the status quo. It means confronting the fear of the unknown and embracing the possibility of change. Here's where the body's fight-or-flight response kicks in, warning us of potential risks and "don't go there". Yet, growth and expansion and living up to our full potential often lies beyond our comfort zones. By consciously and courageously cultivating a sense of feeling safe and secure with exploring the unknown, and assuring ourselves that it is indeed OK to navigate new and unexplored territory, it can become a gateway to discovering our true purpose.

Fear of Rejection or Failure

Rejection doesn't mean that what you have to offer isn't valuable, it just means that you are trying to give it to the wrong person
- **Monica Berg.**

A common fear we can have when exploring life's purpose is the fear of rejection or failure. Merely contemplating something different or sharing new ideas can trigger thoughts of disapproval. We worry that others won't support us or that we'll face criticism. Like a story, the late Bob Proctor told one time; he had an exciting vision and idea of starting his own personal development business after working with Earl Nightingale for several years. He recorded some ideas he had and wanted to share them with a friend to possibly get some reassurance and support in fine-tuning the vision. Bob played the audio to his friend, and as his friend listened to it, Bob felt a strong negative reaction from his friend. So, he stopped playing the audio and said to his friend, "Well, that was just an idea anyway," and he left. As he was driving home, Bob thought: "Wait a minute, that's my idea, and I'm not going to let this person kill my idea. I'm going ahead with it anyway. It's my idea, and it's what I want to do." And the rest is history - Bob Proctor name is legendary in the personal development world today. Don't let the fear of rejection by others, or the fear of failure stifle your ideas and ambitions. Your life's purpose and your visions and goals are all yours to explore, play around with, and execute if you decide to, whether others understand, or agree with them or not.

External Pressures

What other people think of me is none of my business. One of the highest places you can get to, is to be independent of the opinions of other people – Wayne Dyer.

External pressures, particularly from social media platforms, can heavily influence our emotions, our self-concept, and ultimately our decisions. Many are paralysed from speaking up or taking action for fear of what others will think, especially if they are embracing, or aligning with something different and non-mainstream. Frequently heard comments such as "What's with all this spiritual and metaphysical weirdness?" or "Why don't you be normal like the rest of us?" or "Be practical, be realistic" are commonplace comments thrown at those who are exploring new or different paths. But as Bernard Baruch quoted, *"Those Who Mind Don't Matter, and Those Who Matter Don't Mind."* At the end of the day, authenticity garners more respect than conformity. As you discover your mission in life, decide to do it, love it, and enjoy it, and people will respect you more for taking that action, rather than disempowering yourself and backing out because of what you think others might think about you.

Lack of Self-confidence and Self-worth

If you hear a voice within you say, 'you cannot paint,' then by all means paint, and that voice will be silenced
– Vincent Van Gogh.

Many people underestimate themselves and their abilities, and place themselves very low on the 1-10 scale when it comes to self-worth and self-confidence. This self-imposed lack of self-confidence and self-worth is especially true if it is a new experience, or a new venture being considered. Comparing negatively with others who are already experts and professionals tends to make you want to push the "give up before you start" button. There's always a big learning curve in the beginning, but everyone who's successful at something once started from scratch. Self-confidence and self-worth are not necessarily attributes you have to have before you start. Just go ahead take that first step in the direction you know you should go in, and as you move forward, watch your confidence and self-worth grow with each step. It happens automatically with experience. Never let thoughts of lack or less-than stop you from stepping into your life's purpose.

Opting Out of the Hamster Wheel Lifestyle

> *The reasonable man adapts himself to the world; the unreasonable one persists to adapt the world to himself. Therefore, all progress depends on the unreasonable man -*
> **George Bernard Shaw.**

It's easy to get caught up in the routine of daily life—busy with work, career, family, and social obligations—without pausing to reflect on our life's direction. Many drift through life avoiding intentional decision-making as much as possible, and instead merely reacting to everyday circumstances and whatever life throws at them. The demands of daily life can sometimes pull you in many different directions, making it hard to discern what's important and what really matters. If you're doing something because that's what you've always done, or that's what your parents did, or that's what you're trained to do, or it's what you're "supposed" to do, it would be wise to stop and notice what's going on and be open to asking yourself a few questions. Hop off the hamster wheel, park it for a while, and observe what is happening with your life and where you're headed. Are you on track and on purpose with your life's journey, or are you going around in circles? Take a look.

Procrastination vs Making a Decision to Do it Now

The scholar's greatest weakness: calling procrastination research
- **Stephen King**

All you have to work with is this moment - right here, right now. The past has slipped away, and the future has yet to unfold. Procrastination, with its promise of "I'll do it tomorrow," holds no sway when you realize that tomorrow is merely an intangible concept. All you truly possess is the present, and within it lies the seeds of decisive action. Whenever you feel or sense an idea, or a spark ignites within you out of nowhere, you need to trust that it is the universe nudging you to act now. Even the smallest step or decision, such as jotting down a thought on paper, can serve as a catalyst to start you moving in a new direction. In this moment, you hold the power to take responsibility a make decision that could change your life forever. Procrastination, that silent thief of dreams, thrives on the illusion of a tomorrow that never happens. Commit to living in the present moment and taking immediate action on those nudges and gut feelings – that still small voice that you sense in your heart. Do it now. As Paulo Coelho famously said: *One day you will wake up and there won't be any more time to do the things you've always wanted. Do it now.*

Lack of Clarity and Direction

If you don't know where you're going, any road will take you there - Cheshire Cat – **Alice in Wonderland.**

This simple, but convincing, type of reasoning is somewhat related to procrastination - it's another form of excuse. You say, "I can't move forward because I don't know exactly what I'm meant to do, or how I'm meant to do it. I'm not even clear on what my purpose is." Clarity is not a prerequisite for action; but it is often illuminated with momentum. Sometimes, we're compelled to move in a certain direction with very little to go on. It may be just a hunch we have, an intuitive spark with not even a shred of physical evidence, but as we take a step in that direction, more clarity emerges, and the path becomes clearer. There are many examples of how taking those little steps, in spite of the lack of clarity, resulted in massive success stories. Consider Sara Blakely, the founder of Spandex: She wasn't very clear about the solution, but she was curious and determined to make a way that panty lines wouldn't be seen through a dress. She took a little action, did some research and experiments, talked about it, and the solution started to emerge. She definitely didn't have a lot of clarity or direction to begin with, but now Spandex is a multimillion-dollar global industry. In the same vein, our journey towards getting clarity on our purpose may involve following some intuitive guidance and hunches and somewhat vague feelings to begin with. Take the leap, follow those intuitive hunches, and allow the clarity and direction to unfold naturally.

Current Occupation and/or Skills

Beaten paths are for beaten men - **Eric Johnson.**

It is easy to become trapped in the comfort of familiarity and known ways of our current career or the life that we're living because it's working to a degree. We might think, "It's paying the bills, and we're getting by, so why try out anything new or different? Why do I need to consider a change? I'm doing okay; I'm surviving." While some existing occupations and learned skills can indeed align with our life's purpose, it is prudent not to blindly assume this is the case. Perhaps societal pressures or family expectations have shaped your trajectory thus far, leading you to decide on mediocrity and a "normal" occupation and lifestyle as acceptable. True fulfillment often eludes those who settle for the path of least resistance. Your present job or career should not merely sustain you financially but should also be an integral part of achieving your life's purpose if you are planning on staying with it over the long haul. Don't lock yourself into your present situation, if it falls short of aligning with your true values and ambitions. Stay open to new opportunities coming your way

Victim Mentality

> *The difference between a professional victim and an empowered person is not what has happened to them, but the way in which they react to what has happened to them —*
> **Miya Yamanouchi, Author of Embrace Your Sexual Self: A Practical Guide for Women**

Many people get caught up in feeling like a victim, finding comfort in making excuses for their situation and settling there rather than moving forward and actively discovering and living their best life. There are so many diseases and hurtful trauma stories out there that you can use to define your situation and thereby comfortably live your life as a victim and not really expect anything special to happen in your life. By playing the victim role and blaming others, you put the responsibility on somebody else, which means your hands are tied, and you have relinquished the power to do anything about it yourself. However, if you can consciously choose to take full responsibility for your life and then start feeling and acting accordingly, you can break free from being a victim. Whether it's forgiving someone, forgiving yourself, or letting go of the past and detaching yourself from the hurtful situation, you'll start to get your power back again and realize that you do indeed have the power to shape your own life, no matter what has happened in the past. I realize this is often easier said than done, and you may need help in doing it, but it is well worth the effort. Recognizing that you can do it is a good starting point.

Note: In the case of life trauma and suffering imposed situations, or any situation where you feel powerless, please seek professional help, advice, and/or therapy. Anything written here or anywhere in this book should not be taken as a replacement for medical, clinical, or professional advice, diagnosis, or medical intervention.

Lack of Self-love and Self-care

Self-love, my liege, is not so vile a sin, as self-neglecting
— **William Shakespeare.**

While often brushed aside as cliché, these values are fundamental to your overall well-being. They are foundational pieces to building a life of purpose and fulfillment. Some symptoms of a lack of self-love include low energy, low self-esteem and self-worth, feelings of hopelessness, and other negative thoughts often based on false beliefs or assumptions we have believed about ourselves. Coming from a place like this, regardless of how benevolent your intentions are, is not conducive to creativity and living your best life. After all, who wants to see someone doing good things for others but struggling internally to accept themselves? Feeling good about yourself and confident in your abilities is a prerequisite to discovering your life's purpose. Much like the old adage about filling our own "love cup," - you must tend to your own well-being first in order to have enough to share with others. Enjoying your life, relaxing, having fun and laughing often, and even pampering yourself, are all conducive to living your life on a higher vibration where your purpose and mission will become more evident. You need to embrace who you are, flaws and all, and treat yourself with the same kindness and compassion you would offer to a dear friend. I often think how that Bible verse which says "love thy neighbour as thyself" could never have been written by an empath, as we empaths naturally think more of helping others even to the neglect of caring for ourselves. It is the empaths and compassionate souls, more any anyone else, who must not neglect the importance of self-care and self-love in discovering their mission in life.

It's too Risky, and I'll Never Make Money Living My Life's Purpose.

> *People who don't take risks generally make about two big mistakes a year. People who do take risks generally make about two big mistakes a year.* **– Peter F. Drucker.**

There is a pervasive belief that the pursuit of our life's purpose is antithetical to financial prosperity. How often do people lock themselves to mundane occupations, fearing that it is too risky to try something else, thinking that living their passions will lead them astray? We often hear, "Well, my present job is paying the bills, so why change?" or "If I start exploring my life's purpose and discovering what I really love to do, it's never going to pay the bills." Yet, in this fear lies a profound misconception – that the Universe is indifferent to our passions and not interested in us becoming all that we can become. If you have never tried something or taken action in the direction of living your dreams, how do you know it's not going to work? In fact, the odds are stacked in favour of it working simply because you are on purpose and living your life the way you're meant to. It's risky either way, and the bigger risk is that if you don't try something different, you'll miss out and won't get what you really want out of your life. *(For more on this, see "Take a Chance on Me" page 83).* Allow yourself to explore some of the riskier options outside your comfort zone!

Living Your Life's Purpose

You will either step forward into growth or you will step back into safety – **Abraham Maslow.**

Now that you have discovered your purpose in life, or at least you have some pretty good ideas of the direction it is meant to take, it's time to start living it. For some, this path may be crystal clear, a new and exciting direction with the resources, time, and opportunities already aligned. Go for it and make that dream a reality! However, for most, it may involve a slower transition from where you are and what you are doing now, to living a purpose-driven life. The main thing is don't lose sight of your compass point - your true north. Know where you're headed, keep the vision clear, and make choices that serve your purpose. Eventually, your life will become aligned, and most of your dreams and wishes will steadily materialize. Here are a few ideas that I have found helpful in my life and in the lives of those I have coached and interacted with over the years.

Power of Intention

When you change the way you look at things, the things you look at change. The way you perceive things is an extremely powerful tool
— **Wayne Dyer.**

Being a long-time student of Wayne Dyer, I could not discuss the Power of Intention here without referring to his book by the same name. He redefined intention in this book, not as it is generally viewed as this "pit-bull" kind of determination propelling one to succeed at all costs by never giving up on a goal. Instead, he views it as a power in the universe that allows the act of creation to unfold – not as something we do alone, but as an energy we are a part of and allow into our lives as we co-create with this Invisible Power. I love this recent *"Notes from the Universe"* email by Mike Dooley:

Life is not what you see, but what you've projected.
It's not what you've been told, but what you've decided.
And it's not who's appeared, but who you've summoned.
It's not what you've forged, but what you've allowed.

We can set our intentions and know they are being realized because we are aligned and connected with the Power of Intention itself. It is not something we are trying to force into being or convince the Universe to make it happen. Yes, you may need to do your part and use your will to hold the intent in place, stay focused on it in your mind and heart, and not allow the ever-changing outside circumstances around you to try to convince you otherwise. But it's not about hustle and grind, or applying outward physical force; it's about doing the inner work. It's assuming the intention is already realized, and it is just a matter of allowing it to show up in our physical reality. As those powerful words from Neville Goddard advise us, *"Live your life in a sublime spirit of confidence and determination; disregard appearances, conditions, in fact all evidence of your senses that deny the fulfillment of your desire. Rest in the assumption that you are already what you want to be, for in that determined assumption, you and your infinite being are merged in creative unity, and with your infinite being, all things are possible."*

Being intentional is a very powerful way to live your life. It's not about vaguely hoping and wishing and "let's see if it happens." It's coming from a place of knowing and believing that this is what is meant to happen in order to live the highest and best version of yourself, congruent and in line with your mission and purpose. I find when I set my intention for something, big or small, and am able to identify it and express it to myself, it gives me clarity, confidence, and a definite purpose. For example, if I am on my way to a meeting, I'll take a minute before I go to set my intention – what I feel is meant to happen. Such as: "I intend to speak up as soon as I get a chance to discuss this important matter. I need to make people aware of what's happening." Even with more commonplace things that we do in our lives, like going out to dinner with our partner, driving the kids to school, or whatever, it's helpful to set intentions beforehand and give a bit of thought and energy to it; otherwise, our lives tend just to drift along, and mediocrity and apathy can so easily set in. Of course, being intentional does not rule out spontaneity and being open to changing and doing things differently. In fact, to the contrary, I find when I am intentional, I am more aware and open to allowing life to unfold in its wonderful, magical ways.

For those of you who use prayer as a tool, something that I find works well is to set an intention and then add a prayer to it, to lock it in. I often do this in the morning when setting my intentions for the day. For example, after I finish my morning meditation and journaling (or whatever I do for my personal time that morning – it changes often), I'll say to myself (or out loud): "My intention today is to do some research and then write more three chapters of my new book. I'll then form that into a prayer by saying "Cause the words to flow easily and enable me to get some really great content for the last chapter, which I'm a bit stuck on at the moment. Guide me in this". The praying aspect may not be something some of you are comfortable with, and that's fine - just do what works best for you. Of course, with praying, I'm not referring to the old school methods of praying to an external, sometimes angry, God who is choosey in granting his favours to some and not others and insists on his subjects pleasing him and begging and supplicating, and all the rest of it. Praying is simply acknowledging and communicating with the Presence within us, the Life Force Energy, the Higher Power that we are connected to and that causes everything to happen that is happening.

Peter Wescombe

Magic of Synchro-destiny and the Law of Attraction

> *From the beginning, I had a sense of destiny, as though my life was assigned to me by fate and had to be fulfilled. This gave me an inner security, and, though I could never prove to myself, it proved itself to me* – **Carl Jung.**

In our quest for synchronicity and alignment with our life's purpose, we can tap into the magic of *Synchro-destiny* and the Law of Attraction. Deepak Chopra coined the term Synchro-destiny to describe the synchronicities that occur when we align with our true path – our purpose and our destiny. Like Julia Cameron says, *"As you move toward your dream, your dream moves toward you."* The key here is to anticipate and expect more to happen than normal. You do what you can, of course - you take the steps, you do the math and plan the strategy, etc., and because you are on purpose and operating in alignment with the laws of the Universe, you can expect a whole lot more. Look for the signs and opportunities – pay attention to them, acknowledge them, and show your appreciation and gratitude - even for seemingly little coincidences that occur. Gratitude is a powerful energy and has a way of attracting more of what you are thankful for to show up. It creates momentum in the direction of your purpose and can literally start shifting things around in your world.

Cleary see and feel the image of what you desire already happening in your mind so that the unseen powers of the Universe can understand precisely what you want. They will conspire to shift things around, and somehow, the resources you need will just seem to appear by coincidence. Miracles happen, magic happens, and you get lucky. Call it what you like. It is just something that transcends the logical, practical, day-to-day "work really hard and you'll eventually succeed" mentality. When you're putting yourself out there and stepping into a higher frequency of positive expectation and gratitude, the game changes. You start expecting things to happen, and they do. You look around in anticipation and notice things are becoming different. You're in the flow. You think, 'My God if that just happened, I'm open to anything being possible now!" As the legendary CNN talk show host Larry King said, *"Those who have succeeded at anything and don't mention luck are kidding themselves."* We need all the help we can get, so why not accept it and stop being so sceptical? *"If one advances confidently in the direction of his dreams, and endeavours to live the life which he has imagined, he will meet with a success unexpected in common hours,"* assures Henry David Thoreau.

Connecting with Source Energy

With God nothing shall be impossible – **Bible - Luke 1:37**

As I discussed in the earlier section, a big part of finding and living on purpose is taking time to be quiet and connect with your Higher Self, God, Source Energy or whatever name you use. There are many ways to do this, and it doesn't matter which method or modality you use. We're attuned to the results, not the method. Whether you like to meditate, chant, pray, yodel, walk in nature, dance or journal, it doesn't matter as long as it aids you in letting go of your mind chatter and brings you into the Presence and Love of the Universe.

Maybe you have created a special sanctuary space – like a peaceful spot in nature, or you have set up a cozy corner at home that is conducive to connecting. You certainly don't have to follow a religious ritual or join a special organization for this to happen - just calming your mind and becoming aware of the Presence is all you need to do. From this space, your perception changes, your cares, worries, and fears dissolve, and all you are left with is love and unlimited creative possibilities. We've all got to find that time to align our souls and "tune our instrument" so that we can play the beautiful music we are destined to be playing. Find a way to connect every day, whether it's in the morning before you start your day, or maybe you have a sacred nighttime routine - or both. Even during the day, if things start going a bit pear-shaped, or getting a bit intense as they sometimes do, train yourself to stop and pull back, rather than just trying to plough through. Find a way to get quiet and connect and take back control. If you are out in public and can't get away, go and sit on the toilet for a while, or just go into your heart and give yourself some love and care. And then, as dear Virginia Wolfe says, *"Arrange whatever pieces come your way."* In other words, take control, make everything line up, and simply tackle one thing at a time from that place of being connected to peace and serenity.

Your Mind is a Good Servant but a Bad Master

> *The intuitive mind is a sacred gift and the rational mind is a faithful servant. We have created a society that honours the servant and has forgotten the gift* – **Albert Einstein.**

Your mind is a marvellous machine akin to the most intricate computer or sophisticated AI technology. Within it resides some very powerful tools and faculties, including imagination, reason, memory, perception, intuition, and the will —all available and at your disposal, for crafting the life you desire. When you use your mind to create the life you want, it serves as your ally. It becomes a wondrous servant, aiding you in manifesting your dreams. The danger is when the mind becomes the master and starts trying to run your life, which is, unfortunately, what happens to many people because the mind often appears to be a very convincing and dominant authority. This illusory authority, often referred to as the ego, is a master of logic and "common sense," basing most of its advice on our habitual past – never relating to our deeper intuitive or heartfelt guidance. It sees its primary job as keeping things the way they are, and the way they have been in the past, warning us of any perceived threats or changes that may take us out of our comfort zone. To harness the mind's power and effectiveness as your servant, you must train it to align with your life's purpose. Picture your consciousness as a vast sky while your thoughts, emotions, and circumstances are mere fleeting, passing clouds. Amidst this ever-changing panorama, your true north—your purpose—remains constant. The key here is not to let the things that your mind brings to your attention affect you and pull you off track – at least not for very long. Keep your compass aligned with your true north, stay on track, and simply use the mind and its seemingly, well-intentioned advice to propel you further forward.

I've discovered with most of my clients and people I interact with that learning to control the mind chatter, or the "monkey mind," as some people refer to it, is the most common hurdle and obstacle to overcome initially. One research project concluded that we humans have around six thousand separate thoughts each day. The alarming thing is that not only are they mostly negative and disempowering, such as thoughts of apprehension of the future and remorse over the past, but they are also on repeat – we keep thinking those same thoughts over and over again!

We can so easily get caught up in our thoughts and begin to think that we are our thoughts, instead of recognising that we are a detached observer who is simply observing our thoughts and the stories we tell ourselves. I like the way Wayne Dyer suggests we deal with our thoughts: *"Think of yourself as a Divine limitless being rather than a person who doesn't have a choice when it comes to your thoughts. Think of yourself as an observer, contemplating and selecting the thoughts that you choose from the never-ending stream of thoughts on your inner screen. Snatch a thought from the running ribbon of thoughts and contemplate it. As you toss it around notice how you feel – sad depressed, happy, frightened and so on. Every thought going by has an imprint on your concept of yourself. First be the observer, then the contemplator. Now become the choice-maker who can consciously decide to put that thought back onto the running stream and pick up a different one. Thoughts will keep appearing on your mental TV screen, but you'll now be choosing the ones you want to focus on, gather, retain, or let go."*

To ensure that your mind is serving you, you need to detach yourself from it and simply be an observer. Observing it from a detached place of awareness. It's not you, and you don't need to get caught up in reacting to all of the unnecessary drama or negative scenarios it can sometimes convincingly present. Instead, allow any unwanted thoughts to simply dissolve and make way for more empowering and creative thoughts that you can then consciously choose. Making these conscious choices to choose which thoughts you want to think and feel, and which ones you want to simply let float on by and dissolve, ensures that your mind is acting as the *faithful servant* is it meant to be, and thereby helping you move you in the direction of your purpose.

There may be times when you are faced with extreme negative thoughts that appear very powerful in a disempowering way. They can be overwhelmingly difficult to control, such as when you receive some bad news, a situation that didn't go as planned, or you are dealing with some urgent issue. In these situations, when the thoughts are charged with strong emotions and feelings, it takes a bigger, conscious effort, and time to work with your body to calm them and get your mind under control. Conscious breathing is usually a good first step, along with giving yourself some time and working with your body to regain control. Always be gentle and never harsh with yourself. Consider also seeking professional help and/or therapy in certain cases as your best course of action.

Overcoming Limiting Mindsets and Changing the Concept You Have of Yourself

When you are inspired by some great purpose, some extraordinary project, all your thoughts break their bonds, your mind transcends its limitation, and your consciousness expands in every direction, and you find yourself in a new and a greater and a wonderful world. Dormant forces, faculties and talents come alive, and you discover yourself to be a greater person by far than you ever dreamed yourself to be – **Patanjali.**

Training our minds to overcome limiting mindsets and limiting beliefs is a big subject and not something that we can cover in the scope of this book. It is an essential component, however, to becoming the best version of yourself and living your life's purpose. The self-image or self-concept that you have of yourself is the primary factor determining the direction your life takes. It controls your mind, your decisions, and, therefore, your results. Your achievements and successes in your life cannot be greater than the image you have of yourself. Your self-image is your conception of the sort of person you are. It determines what you believe you are able to accomplish. This image or opinion you have of yourself will also determine how you interpret other people's reactions to you and, consequently, how you respond.

The personal development industry is filled with many techniques, modalities, and methods to help with this. Tools such as affirmations, auto-suggestions, neuroplasticity, visualization, hypnosis, journalling, meditation, personal coaching and other similar tools to train and recalibrate your brain and your mind can all work if you are consistent with the practices over time. Your brain and your subconscious mind basically operate according to the habits that have been forged over the years. It comprises primarily of things that you have been exposed to and have been repeated enough to form a habit, as well as things that have significantly impacted you enough, either positively or negatively, to create an imprint in your life. This, along with your inherited DNA, forms your existing paradigm, or self-image and belief system from which you perceive life, base your decisions and subsequent actions on. The self-image, or concept you have of yourself is where your current limitations reside – or where your thermostat is set. The illustration of a thermostat is a good way of explaining the way mindsets and paradigms work. You often hear of someone winning the lottery and then they end up losing it all again after a few years. That's because their thermostat is set on a certain level of wealth or success. And even if it does increase, it eventually gets back to the "safe" thermostat setting that they have set for themselves because of the way they have lived for most of their life. It can be the same with someone who goes on a weight loss program. They initially lose a few kilos, but they don't stick at it, and eventually, they get back to the thermostat setting of their previous weight levels. This whole principle is explained very well in a book called *Psycho-Cybernetics by Maxwell Waltz*.

Just as those habits and impactful things from the past have created your current self-image and set the thermostat at its existing setting, it can just as easily be changed and reset by introducing different actions to train our mind and brain and form new and different habits.

Changing and improving your self-image is a choice you can make any time you choose to, and no one can stop you from changing it. The degree to which you improve your image of yourself will be in direct proportion to how much you believe that you can honestly accept about yourself, as well as the amount of effort you put into upgrading your new self-image.

(Note: Feel free to contact us via the email address given at the beginning of this book if you want more help and support in this area)

Transitioning from Where you Are to Where you Want to Be

We cannot solve our problems with the same thinking we used when we created them - **Albert Einstein.**

Transitioning from where you are to where you want to be can look like a daunting leap and, if it means grinding it out and working tirelessly on the physical plane only, then it indeed would be. But living our dream and becoming who we are destined to be is largely an inside job. Many have said it is about 80% inner work (the why) and 20% outside action work (the how). What you desire already exists on a different frequency, a different realm. It's a bit like those fascinating optical illusions where you look at the picture initially and see one image only, and then by slightly tilting the picture or adjusting your vision, it transforms into another completely different image. The other image was there all the time, but you didn't see it until you made a slight change in your perception or your position of view. Like that famous optical illusion image of a young woman and an ugly old woman.

Example of an Optical illusion image

Similarly, everything you aspire to achieve or become is already present and in existence, awaiting your awareness of it and your action to bring it into visible reality. This notion aligns with the concept of living from the end, a successful approach suggested and emphasized by most manifesting experts and success coaches. It involves vividly visualizing your desired outcome and feeling how it feels when it's already accomplished. This isn't about pretending or faking it; rather, it's about recognizing the reality of your vision, being thankful for it, and acting as though it was already in existence.

Like the Wright Brothers envisioned themselves flying and soaring through the skies long before it actually happened, they lived from the end, persistently visualizing their success until it materialized. Similarly, winning athletes often visualize victory, picturing themselves crossing the finish line or claiming gold medals. This practice of seeing from the end and embracing the feelings and emotions of it as already accomplished is a common thread among those who accomplish remarkable feats.

Defining, visualizing and feeling your desired reality clearly is essential for transitioning towards it. Write it down, create a vision board, use affirmations, immerse yourself in the feeling of already being there. Do whatever it takes – both internally and externally! Mentally enjoy driving in the car you wish to own (or, better still, actually test drive it), explore the house you envision living in. Study the habits of those who've successfully achieved what you seek. By embodying and feeling your desired reality in your mind, you naturally begin moving towards it, and it begins to move towards you.

As you focus your attention on your aspirations, you'll notice synchronicities and opportunities start aligning with your intentions. Just as you start seeing real silver BMW cars everywhere once you've decided on buying a silver BMW. The universe responds to your focused attention. The silver BMWs were there all the time, you just never noticed them until you started focussing on them. Spend time visualizing, imagining and embracing the feeling of already being where you want to be.

By focusing persistently and intently on experiencing the feelings of how it would feel to be or have what you envision, you create energy and power within yourself as well as attractive power on the outside. For example, if one million dollars is what you want in order to get underway with your life's purpose, try seeing yourself paying the home mortgage off and feeling what it is like to tell your partner or close friends that you are paying it off and how wonderful it feels to have the cash available. Feel how proud you are of yourself for staying thankful - believing and knowing it was happening back then when you had nothing. Feel proud of yourself for the way you insisted on "living from the end" back then and not giving up. See yourself transferring large amounts of money in your bank and buying things you had in mind to buy while you were waiting for the money to materialize, etc. Do this inner work often – consider setting an hourly chime to notify you to take a minute to two every hour, whenever suitable, to feel into it. The more you do it, the more natural it will feel, and the sooner you will start to see your outer world shaping itself upon the model of your new reality.

There's a verse in the Bible that says, "Faith is the substance of things hoped for." Apparently, the word "substance" was translated from the original Greek word for property title deed – or proof of ownership. Faith is the proof of the ownership of what you want. You may have never seen the property physically, but having the title deed for it ensures it's yours. You believe it. You know you own it, and you will see it eventually.

Nelson Mandela was locked in a maximum-security prison on Robben Island for 15 years, feeling completely hopeless and thinking that his dream and vision of leading his country to freedom would never happen. He explained that one day he allowed himself to entertain the new thought of "maybe this is how it looks while it is happening". It was shortly after that he was led to begin writing letters. He used this method of communication to garner support from the media and various influential people for the end of apartheid. And the rest is history.

Make the transitioning process from where you are now, to the life you envision living, a relentless pursuit, using whatever tools and resources you have available - both inner and outer.

Additional Notes on Transitioning: An important consideration when contemplating how to get from where you are to where you want to be is the financial ramifications. Getting to where you want to be and living your dream will probably be something that you want to happen as quickly as possible. There will, no doubt, be some important decisions to make moving forward. You could consider transitioning with one huge leap, or it may need to happen over a long time. You

Unpacking Your Life's Purpose

know what's best, and you know what you're capable of. If you're struggling financially, for example, you may need to keep your existing job for a while longer until you are able to make your new job, or your new vocation, pay financially. You may have other people in your life – a partner and children and/or other factors to take into consideration. I've known some people who decided that they were not living their life's purpose, so they immediately finished up with their current paying job and jumped full on into their dream, only to discover that it's taken longer than they thought to get it up and running. As a result, they ended up becoming overly consumed and stressed about getting the money for their day-to-day survival needs, so they've just given up on their dream and gone back to their paying job. It's not necessarily the best idea to drop everything and jump full-on into living your dream and purpose, although it can be very appealing to do so initially. Having no money can be very stressful and draining. In this case, it's sometimes better to start by giving some of your time to creating and building your dream while keeping your present job so you don't have to worry about finding money to pay the bills during the transition. If you really mean business, you'll be willing to sacrifice a few time and/or possibly money-related things, that are not essential so that you can build your dream. "Sacrifice" here meaning to give up something of a lower nature in order to bring in something of a higher nature. For example, you let go of some bad food habits so that you can start building a healthier lifestyle or let go of an old relationship that you know is not working so you can start a looking for a new relationship. Sit down and take stock and see what you can give up financially or timewise so that you can maximize your focus on creating the life of your dreams and fulfilling your purpose.

Take a Chance on Me – How Risky Is It Really?

> *Reality is largely negotiable. If you stress-test the boundaries and experiment with the "impossibles," you'll quickly discover that most limitations are a fragile collection of socially reinforced rules you can choose to break at any time*
> **- Tim Ferris.**

Price Prichard has a very good book titled *You Squared*. It's a short 36 page read in which he lays out some very empowering quantum leap strategies for stepping out of our comfort zones to achieve exponential growth and success. He quotes Fred Alan Wolfe's description of a quantum leap from his award-winning book Taking the Quantum Leap: *"A quantum leap is… the explosive jump that a particle of matter undergoes in moving from one place to another … in a figurative sense, taking a quantum leap means taking a risk, going off into an unchartered territory with no guide to follow"* Pritchett adds: *"Physicists studying quantum mechanics note that particles make these "jumps" without apparent effort and without covering all the bases between the starting and ending points."*

In a later chapter titled: *Choose a Different Set of Risks*, Pritchett elaborates further: *The risks hit you as rather apparent and may be quite threatening, but you must stack them up against the hidden risks you accept when you decide to live with the status quo. Ask yourself what you are risking if you do not go for the quantum leap. The risk is that you won't get what you want out of life... Risk believing in yourself—risk acting on the assumption that you can succeed in making a quantum leap. Otherwise, the risk is that you settle for only a fraction of what life has to give you. This isn't a case of taking a big chance. It's a matter of giving yourself a chance."*

Allow yourself to try different things, to experiment, and to take steps into the unknown if the situation warrants it. And don't wait until all the lights are green before taking action. Procrastination and excuses, and probably plenty of well-meaning advisors, will be right there at this juncture to convince you otherwise, but there will never be a perfect time to do so. I'll finish this section with another passage from Price Pritchett in his chapter Make Your Move Before You're Ready: *"...you don't "prepare" for a quantum leap. You make it and then fine-tune your approach. You go for it instead of forever getting ready... Move on to your dream ... start ...and let what happens help you develop a coherent game plan... You'll discover, once underway, that you know more than you know you know. Trust your instincts. ... A quantum leap is a move that is yours for the taking. Right now. It represents a giant step that you can make merely by deciding to and opening yourself up to the resources presently available to serve you."*

To truly manifest our dreams, we must be willing to take the step. As Richard Branson famously quipped, *"Screw it, let's do it."* Remember, we only live once, so why not live boldly, authentically, unapologetically? As Alfred Adler put it so well, *"The chief danger in life is that you may take too many precautions."* Dare to dream, dare to explore, and dare to live on purpose. Your life is waiting to be transformed.

Peter Wescombe

Making Decisions and 7 Ways to Test Your Decision

Decisions, or lack of them are responsible for making or breaking everything you desire in life. People who have become very proficient at making decisions, without being influenced by the opinions of others, are the same people whose annual incomes fall into the top income category - **Napoleon Hill.**

Deciding is not merely a choice; if it's a committed decision, it's a call to action. Each decision we make sets a course, propelling us forward on the journey of our lives. Yet, how often do we find ourselves hesitating, waiting for the perfect moment, the ideal circumstances? We wait for the stars to align, for the money to materialize, and for the right people to appear. But in truth, the power lies in making the decision itself.

It's about shifting your perspective from one of hesitation to one of expectancy and then initiating action by making a committed decision. Make the decision and watch as the universe conspires to support you. Trust that the resources, the people, and the opportunities will align with your path. And even if they don't, see it as an opportunity, a chance to recalibrate or tweak a bit and decide again. The key is to keep moving forward, one decision at a time.

Research has shown that highly successful people tend to make decisions quickly and change them very slowly, if and when they are changed at all. By comparison, people who are rarely successful tend to make decisions very slowly, and they change their decisions very quickly and often. They generally have the habit of being influenced in their decision-making by the opinions of others, while successful people stay aligned with their own purpose and direction.

Good decision-makers usually have a high degree of self-confidence. Learning to become proficient at decision-making is a skill well worth developing. Start right where you are with whatever you've got and practice making clear and intentional decisions. Confident decision-makers know exactly what they want. They make a decision and from that point onwards, it is a done deal. It's just a matter of time before it materializes, even if the decision made runs contrary to the existing current circumstances or visible resources. People have a way of standing by their decision once it is made and will somehow come up with the money or resources needed to support it, even if it looks impossible initially. That's the power of making committed decisions.

Here are 7 ways to know if your decision is the right one for you and aligned with your life's calling or purpose. The first 4 are inner ways, and the last 3 are outer ways. If you are preparing to make a decision, try being completely open and detached and see how it lines up with these.

1. Aligned with Your Beliefs: Is it aligned with all that you believe and value and what matters to you? It is unlikely you will be guided to do something that you do not believe in, or that is contrary to your values. For example, suppose your beliefs and values are in the area of promoting organic living and caring for the planet and the environment. In that case, it is unlikely

that a job at a chemical pesticide company would be the direction you are being guided to take.

2. The Voice of Words: You may be casually reading or listening to something, or contemplating an idea or thought pattern and all of a sudden, you are reminded of a quote, or a line of a song, or some words from a poem. It just drops into your mind out of nowhere, and it's like: "Whoa, where did that come from! That's it! That's for me." It may be something unrelated to what you were reading or thinking about, but the quote or passage comes through loud and clear and lights up your whole world, and bang! That's it. The decision and path ahead is now clear and certain. Or, sometimes, it can be a noticeable thread of quotes and passages on the same theme or subject that seem to be consistently showing up in everything that you are reading, or noticing on social media threads, or in what people are talking to you about. For example, you are a healing practitioner and are considering making a decision to start a series of regular healing retreats. Everything you have been reading is pointing in this direction and telling you to step out and use your gifts and talents. Later, when having a shower, totally detached from thinking about anything in particular, a key paragraph from a book you were reading last week just popped into your mind out of nowhere, totally aligned with your decision, and you just know it's a confirmation that you are on track with this decision. There is no doubt about it.

3. The Voice of Your Conscience and Intuition: Sometimes, our feelings can be fleeting and shallow and quite changeable. But if it is coming from your heart and soul, you will have an inner conviction, an unshakable feeling of certainty and knowing. It totally feels right. It's that still small voice in your heart – not necessarily out loud, not an audible, visible sign of any kind. It's your "gut feeling," as some people call it, or your intuition. It's coming your heart, and you just know that it's what you are supposed to do. In fact, you may even start feeling a little uneasy and uncomfortable whenever you try to move away from it and stop thinking about it. Some people, and especially women, seem to be more attuned to this divine feminine attribute than others, but it is learnable trait and well worth cultivating and developing.

4. Direct Guidance: This can be in the form of a vivid dream in the night that contains clear direction and guidance. Or it can be an impressionable vision or picture that comes to mind in your waking hours, that you can't seem to stop thinking about. Alternatively, some people are good at channelling and receiving direct messages and communications from the other realm - maybe a departed loved one gets through with a message, or you feel a strong presence of a being from the world of spirit bringing some guidance. Or you simply have a strong awareness of your higher self-connecting with Universal Presence, bringing a personal message. The Universe has a way of causing this type of guidance to be so "tailor made", and

uniquely suited to you that you are totally convinced of its authenticity and certainty, and you act accordingly.

5. **Confirmed by Trusted Advisors:** Although nobody else can truly know what's best for you, during the decision-making time, it's often helpful to bounce things off someone(s) who you trust and who may offer some different perspectives, or to simply encourage you that they are seeing your proposed decision as the highest and best for you. Of course, the emphasis here is on a trusted advisor – meaning someone who you know, by their actions and results, are on a similar, or higher frequency, than you are and have your best interests in mind. However, the final decision has to be made by you and you alone - because only you can truly know and believe what it is the best for you.

6. **Conditions and Circumstances (aka Open and Closed Doors)** While the Universe can certainly shuffle things around for us in the outer world to align with our inner purpose and goals, the current circumstances are temporary and always changing and not necessarily a sure way of judging or deciding what we should do. But they can serve as an indication or as a confirmation. Where does it appear that the lights are red or doors are closing, and where does it look like green lights and open doors of opportunity? For example, if your neighbours have started causing problems and you are not enjoying where you currently live, and you have just received an invitation to work with a long-time friend in another city. It could be an indication and a confirmation of your decision to move to that new city.

7. Confirming Signs: Some people can trust in this more than others, and although not necessarily a strong base for making a decision, it can be a helpful and convincing confirmation, either just prior to making the decision or as a confirmation once the decision has been made. This can be intentionally requested, such as asking the Universe to provide a specific sign to show you are on the right track. For example, you demand that tickets be available within a certain time frame for the travel you will need to make to accomplish your decision. Or, instead of intentionally demanding a certain thing to happen as a confirmation, you can simply notice confirming things along the way. For example, you know from previous happenings that as a good luck omen or a sign of God's presence with you, you'll often see a blue butterfly when you are on track with your purpose, or you always see combinations of the number 11 - or whatever it is for you. These signs are always so encouraging.

Be You - Be Unstoppable - Be Obsessed!

It is a funny thing about life; if you refuse to accept anything but the best you very often get it - **W. Somerset Maugham.**

We've all heard the well-known quote by Oscar Wilde: *"Be you, everyone else is taken."* That's one of the main themes throughout this book. It's all about living your purpose – not anyone else's, or according to what you think someone else is expecting of you. Once you know your mission and purpose in life, find a way to make it happen, and don't let anything or anyone stop you from achieving it! Ups and downs, open doors and closed doors, good days and bad days are all "par for the course" on your journey. Like the pathway to get to the mountaintop - it's never a straight line. Dear Marie Foleo aptly reminds us in her book of the same name that *"Everything is figureoutable."* No matter how insurmountable a problem may appear, if the fulfillment of your life's purpose is on the other side of it, then there must be a way either through it, over it, under it, or around it – or maybe just give it some time and the problem will dissolve and disappear. Everything in this physical world is changing all the time. And what may seem impossible today, after a good night's sleep and a fresh start in the morning, solutions and answers all of a sudden appear, and it's all green lights. It's a co-creation process, like the old saying I learnt in my missionary cult days says: *"You do what you can do, and God will do what you can't do,"* The wonderful thing is that you can know and trust that the Universe has your back when you are on purpose and aligned with your divine mission in life. Those "lucky breaks" and unexpected coincidences seem to become more commonplace.

Being unstoppable, however, does not mean constantly working hard, grinding and hustling and stressing. Long gone are the "old school" masculine energy philosophies of only using brute force, physical hard work, and long stressful hours as the way to accomplish anything. To the contrary, finding a balance and engaging some of our feminine energies such as creativity, intuitive and "out of the box" ideas, trusting and slowing things down to observe what is happening from a different perspective, seeking advice, etc., will not only cause a better result and outcome, but it will also make the process more enjoyable and much less burn out along the way. A lot of self-love and self-care philosophy is about enjoying the journey, enjoying life, and not always being so results-focused. It wouldn't hurt to ask ourselves Tim Ferris's question more often when faced with a daunting task: *"What would this look like if it were easy?"*

Doing what you love and what you are passionate about matters a whole lot and can be the impetus that keeps you going in the direction of your life's purpose when everything else seems contrary. But it takes more than that – it takes an obsession. Obsession goes beyond passion. Obsession is about total commitment. It's that *"the burning desire for your magnificent obsession"* It's the voice inside that echoes: *"I'm going there, and nothing will stop me."* It's the unwavering resolve to see it through, no matter what, regardless of what discomfort, doubts, or waning enthusiasm tries to creep in. There will be times when you question everything, when the love and passion for your pursuit seems to flicker. But obsession causes you to remain true to your decision because your commitment is set. Your mind may scream, "It's not working. It's not for me. I've had enough. Let's try something else" Being obsessed doesn't listen; instead, it faithfully, consistently, persistently, and confidently keeps going, keeps moving forward until it happens.

Like the story of the tribe in Africa, which had a 100% success rate with its rain dances: In order to discover the secret of the success of this particular tribe, anthropologists compared this tribe with other rain dance tribes in the region that were not always successful. The anthropologists couldn't find any differences. They all had similar costumes, prayed and chanted similar incantations and performed similar rituals. Like all the tribes, this tribe sometimes danced for weeks on end. Finally, a very astute observer noticed one significantly distinct difference. The successful tribe always danced until it rained!

Be unstoppable, be obsessed, and ***"dance until it rains"!***

Listening to Your Body and Its Feelings

It is important to listen to your heart, your inner voice, your intuition, as well as your bodily sensations and your nervous system, all of which can serve as invaluable guidance, offering insights into your life's direction. That slight wave of uneasiness and anxiety, or that unexpected thought or concern is showing up for a reason. Listen to those sensations, draw them out, and see what's going on. Those old, outdated modalities of resisting all negative thoughts and refusing to accept anything that's not upbeat and positive are akin to old-school Christianity of "rebuking the devil" and resisting those "evil" thoughts whenever something a bit contrary or different emerges. It's very antiquated, and as the saying goes: "what you resist persists." Try welcoming these sensations, listening to your body and nervous system more. Practice being more loving, gentle, and kinder with yourself and not so harsh and forceful, especially if you are struggling with feelings of anxiety, stress, uneasiness or overwhelm of some form. There are some very helpful, self-applicable techniques and psychosensory therapies available these days, such as Havening (this involves gently rubbing and massaging certain points of the body - hands, arms, forehead, under eyes, etc.), and also Tapping or EFT (Emotional Freedom Technique), which involves gently tapping different meridians in your body to help release anxiety or particular things you may be going through. Of course, talking with a trusted friend, mentor, or therapist can also be very helpful. Or, if the situation warrants it, consult a professional doctor or therapist.

Purpose, Visions, Goals, and Plans – How Does it All Fit Together?

Decide what you want.
Decide what you are prepared to give up, to get it.
Set your mind to it.
Get on with the work.

-H.L. Hunt

Once you've discovered your purpose, you can then start expressing it by first creating a vision. Your vision is what you see happening in your life. It's the strategy behind the fulfillment of your purpose. You set the vision in motion and accomplish it by creating several short-term goals to keep you on course. Like Van Gogh famously said: *"I dream my painting, and I paint my dream."* He knew his purpose in life, and his vision then was the completion of paintings, each uniquely different from the other. The way he put his vision onto canvas involved a series of short-term goals. The vision is the key connector between setting your goals and your life's purpose.

For example, a part of your life's *purpose* could be helping people to respect our planet by aligning and bonding with nature. And in order to do this, you have created a vision of setting up a retreat in a certain area of your country. The initial *goal* could be to purchase some land in this specific area and start living there by the end of this year. Then, coming up with specific step by step *plans* on how to reach the goal becomes the short-term focus – strategies on how to make the move, how to get the financing etc.

Purpose: Your "Dharma" - your highest calling. The ultimate mission and reason for your life. Your truest path to your fulfillment.

Visions: Physical embodiments of your purpose. Created and dreamed up from your imagination and your hearts desires as the ideal possibilities and scenarios for your purpose to be manifested. Your visions can be long term such as your lifelong dreams, or shorter-term such as your vision of where you intend to be within the next 3-5 years.

Goals: These are the series of steps needed in order to accomplish and fulfill the vision. It's plotting the course. For example, if your vision is to grow your new business revenue to a million dollar within 3 years, then your goals will be the steps that will be required for you to get it there.

Plans: The plans are your blueprints that you draw up to give you the specific tasks and action steps that you need to take to accomplish the goals. It's where the "rubber meets the road" Plans can be intricately detailed - complete with spreadsheets and accurate to-scale drawings, or they can be a few simple notes to refer to, as you move forward. Whatever works best for you is how you plan.

The journey towards realizing your visions and reaching your goals will, no doubt, be an adventure and certainly not a direct straight line. "Life happens" as they say, along the way, but your commitment is to stay true to your north star and allow yourself to be guided moment by moment and day by day from your inner compass. Outside contrary circumstances and unplanned events and situations will sometimes arise to test your resolve and fortitude but always keep in mind that you are greater than the temporary circumstances or setbacks and you can use them as stepping stones rather than stumbling blocks. Whenever things seem to begin to go awry, just stop for a minute, step back, take a deep breath and ask yourself some empowering questions like *"I wonder what I can do to change this situation? What happens next here? How can I make this easier, simpler, better, different?"* Bring in a bit of flexibility, resourcefulness, creativity, awareness, advice from others, research, reasoning – whatever it takes to get the momentum up again and "you're off to the races."

Assessing Your Progress

Success is the progressive realization of a worthy ideal
- **Earl Nightingale.**

Staying on purpose and keeping the direction and trajectory of your life aligned with your north star is important. You can track and monitor this in many different ways and with different degrees of intensity. Some people may prefer to closely monitor themselves and set up weekly or monthly targets, which they review and tweak regularly. Others may find it works better to give themselves more flexibility and leeway and assess things over a longer period. Either way, there should be times when you step back as an observer and take a good look at your life. This can include revisiting your life's purpose outline, observing how your physical world is aligning with this, noting where changes need to be made, and even doing a major reset if needed.

Having a balanced life in all areas is key. Living your life's purpose is not a personal accomplishment or a physical achievement that must happen regardless of unfavourable results along the way. Rather it's an unfoldment of your beautiful life and the beneficial results should harmonize with, and positively impact, not only your own life but all who come in contact with you. As Dr Peter Attia wrote with raw honesty, in the Epilogue of his book Outlive, *"What I eventually realized after a long and painful journey is that longevity is meaningless if your life sucks. Or your relationships suck. None of it matters if your wife hates you. None of it matters if you are a shitty father, or if you are consumed by anger or addictions. Your resume doesn't really matter either when it comes time for your eulogy"* Getting help and support on your journey from an outside source, such as a personal coach or mentor, a friend or accountability partner who is willing to be honest with you, can be very beneficial. There are also many different life value guides and structures for living a well-balanced life available on the internet that can be used to assess how you are doing. For example, Tony Robbin's 6 basic human needs list, Abraham Maslow's hierarchy of 5 human needs, and Regan Hillyer's 9 categories of wealth, health, contribution, purpose, mindset, emotions, passion, relationships, and spirituality. I like to use a very simple list of 4 pillars that I came across in reading something from Tai Lopez many years ago. These 4 pillars are quite basic but can include every aspect of our lives. His four pillars are:

1. **Health** – This includes physical exercise, nutrition, environment, a positive mental attitude, and anything to do with the care of your body and mind.

2. **Wealth** – This includes money, business, career, and entrepreneurial pursuits.

3. **Love** – This includes family, friends, socializing, self-love and self-care, personal growth, spirituality.

4. **Happiness** – This includes lifestyle, giving, community, contribution

Try choosing one of the different guides above – or make your own list, and then give yourself a rating between 1 and 10 for each pillar. Note areas you are committing to improving on and then do the rating again periodically.

Remember, happiness is not a destination but a way of travelling, so enjoy the journey! It is your life that is unfolding here, and you've only got one chance at it.

Conclusion

Someone dear to my heart suggested I should write a conclusion for this book. My mindset was telling me "You're not good at book conclusions – and besides you've never written one, so why even attempt it" As I observed this bit of negative self-talk that bubbled up, I recognised it as one of those repetitive thoughts that has appeared many times in my past in an effort to keep me seemingly safe, comfortable and "risk-free" in the way I live my life. It's a good example of my mind attempting to be the *"bad master"* instead of the *"good servant"* it is meant to be (as discussed on page 71). So, I decided to follow Wayne Dyer's advice (also on page 71) and *"first be the observer, then the contemplator. Then become the choice-maker who can consciously decide to put that thought back onto the running stream and pick up a different one."* which I did, and the next thought that showed up said, "remember how you didn't think you could do that room renovation last month, but look how wonderful it turned out" I didn't need to contemplate that thought for very long before I recognised it as a more empowering thought, and that it was making me feel good. So, I grabbed it, and it immediately aligned with the suggestion of writing a conclusion for my book. The positive charge of energy in that thought caused me to "grab the bull by the horns" and take action and decide to do it. The decision, and the action that followed, was made by simply choosing which thought I preferred and letting the other one go. They're all just random thoughts until we energize them with a decision and make them real.

Utilizing the material in this book to help you discover and live your life on purpose will work - and it's not rocket science. There is nothing really new or secretive about any of this material. The content and principles are pretty universal and are woven throughout most of humanity's philosophical writings – both ancient and modern day. Those who study religious faiths will also find these principles are there, albeit often buried underneath a lot of man-made rules, traditions and ceremonies that dominate religions these days. Science, now is also confirming and finding measurable proof to support many of these invisible principles of the universe, especially in the fields of philosophy, neuroscience, metaphysics, longevity, psychology, artificial intelligence etc. As you probably noticed, I have quotes and passages sprinkled throughout the book from a large variety of people and sources.

The main problem most people have with embracing and executing this material and taking advantage of the many benefits associated with understanding it, is that it's not mainstream and not accepted by the majority of the population. It's still a bit "out there" and unknown territory and "not-proven" enough for the majority of people to "risk" stepping out. Sure, it takes an element of faith and trust to accept some of these principles and live them from the inside until they manifest in the outside world, but to relinquish control of your destiny and allow the outside world of unpredictable circumstances and events and people to control your life is a much riskier place to put your faith and trust in.

Life is such a precious gift and we have so much to look forward to everyday. Ask anyone who has had an NDE or suffered and survived a life-threatening situation and they'll tell you. Like Ric Elias – who had a front-row seat on the plane that crash-landed in the Hudson River in New York in January 2009 said: *I think people get old when they stop thinking about the future. If you want to find someone's true age – listen to them. If they talk about the past and talk about all the things that happened that they did, they've gotten old. If they think and talk about their dreams and their aspirations, what they're still looking forward to, they're young.* And Ric is right. The key to living our purpose successfully is to "be young" regardless of the number of our age - to think and feel and talk and act like a someone who is energized and enthusiastic about the future, and full of gratitude for the wonderful life that has been given to us to enjoy and share with others.

I'll be turning 68 this year and feel my life is just getting started! My partner and I have so many exciting ideas and plans and visions up ahead. I have just started a new life-coaching career and my partner has just started out to become a professional photographer. Next year we are planning a trip to Nepal and a hike to the Everest base camp. Then we have a wellness retreat to get set up and running on our beautiful property. At the same time, we live calm, relaxed stress-free lives. …. and so can you.

…. that reminds me, I better get started with my next book - it's about longevity.

www.ingramcontent.com/pod-product-compliance
Lightning Source LLC
Chambersburg PA
CBHW052149070526
44585CB00017B/2044